Lanarkshire's Legendary C

by
Bruce Peter

E. H. Bostock's Hamilton Hippodrome opened on 14 October 1907. Bostock was born into an already famous circus family from Buckinghamshire. Apart from lavishly-presented menageries in Portobello and Glasgow, his family's firm, Bostock and Wombwell, also ran several theatres, circuses and cinemas in East Anglia. The Hippodrome was a large, predominantly wooden building which must have looked out of place among the dour sandstone terraces of Townhead Street. The interior had a circle and balcony, and the proscenium and stalls could be removed to make a ring suitable for circus performances. Between the circus visits and regular film shows, the cockney comedienne Lily Morris, comic singer George Formby (senior) and Fred Karno's Gang were big variety attractions. During the thirties, such comedy favourites as Harry Gordon, Dave Willis and Tommy Morgan appeared. The Hippodrome was destroyed by a devastating overnight fire, ironically on Burns' Night in 1946.

First published in the United Kingdom, 1999,
by Stenlake Publishing, Ochiltree Sawmill, The Lade,
Ochiltree, Ayrshire, KA18 2NX
Telephone / Fax: 01290 423114

ISBN 1 84033 068 6

ACKNOWLEDGEMENTS

Thanks to Allen Eyles, Kevin Gooding, Scott McCutcheon, John McKillop and Kevin Wheelan for supplying additional photographs.

THE PUBLISHERS REGRET THAT THEY CANNOT SUPPLY COPIES OF ANY PICTURES FEATURED IN THIS BOOK.

Anyone with photographic or other documentary material relating to Lanarkshire's cinemas is invited to contact the author via the publisher.

In November 1929 the New Century Theatre in Windmillhill Street, Motherwell (page 35), was sold to John Maxwell's ABC company. It was closed and partially demolished in 1933 so that a radical reconstruction could take place. The site was excavated to a depth of twenty feet – right down to the boulder clay – and only the exterior walls and parts of the original facade survived the demolition. The replacement Rex cinema, designed by Charles J. McNair, opened in 1936. The partial cladding of the original frontage in brown and cream bricks was a mistake, especially as the remains of the original lanterns still stuck out of the top. The Rex closed in 1976, and after a spell of dereliction the building became an amusement arcade and night club. That too failed and the remains of the Rex were finally dismantled in the spring of 1995.

INTRODUCTION

When the French inventors, Claude and Auguste Lumire, gave the first ever cinema show in Britain in the Polytechnic Great Hall in London in February 1896, they presented their invention as an important scientific discovery, rather than as mere entertainment. It was, however, variety impresarios and travelling showmen who first realised the commercial potential of the exciting new medium. With its vast coalfields and heavy industry, Lanarkshire had a burgeoning population to be entertained. Many of the first cinema shows in towns and villages in the area were given by the Greens – a Lancashire family who had moved their show ground to Vinegar Hill in Glasgow in search of better fortunes. George Green not only built an early cinema there, but also equipped a collapsible cinema booth, which could be towed from town to town by a steam traction engine. Around the turn of the century, the Palmers, well-known Lesmahagow showmen, equipped their own travelling cinema show. Even then, a distinct attitude to cinema architecture was emerging. Their ingenious booths had ornate neo-baroque facades, illuminated by hundreds of incandescent bulbs; a steam organ played jaunty music and gaily costumed showmen heralded the delights within to lure patrons to enter. Once inside, eager audiences were crammed into rudimentary tented sheds with wooden benches. Much of this carnival razzmatazz clung to the cinema as its status developed and it moved from fairground to town centre to suburb, retaining a vividly uniformed staff, parties, ceremonies, music and brilliant night-time illumination.

At the same time, other cinema entrepreneurs brought their shows to one-night performances in Lanarkshire's many miners' welfare halls. Richard Singleton abandoned his printing business in Rutherglen to enter the prospering cinema trade. His son George, who became an important Scottish cinema magnate, recalled that:

> We would move in and tie up a screen against one wall. The films may have been silent, but nothing else was. The projector was set up in the middle of the audience and it rattled and clanked relentlessly. Those highly flammable nitrate film spools would be lying around on the floor and people would just drop their cigarette ends amongst them. It terrifies me to think of it now, but there were few safety regulations in those days. All the while I walked round with a tray shouting 'caramels, chocolates, toffee!' As the film started, we'd all be plunged into darkness, and my father would thump away on a piano at the side. Babies would cry, conversations would continue, and those who could read would loudly repeat captions for the benefit of the illiterate and short-sighted around them. When a spool broke, everyone would hiss and stamp their feet.

Following a number of serious cinema fires, the government passed the Kinematograph Act in 1909. The issuing of cinema licences ensured that only buildings with isolated fireproof projection boxes, solid steel or concrete frames and adequate fire exits could remain in use. As film quality improved and interest continued to grow, a new generation of purpose-built cinemas was opened. The Wishaw Picture House was typical, with its gaudy entrance fronting a plain brick shed with a pitched metal roof – an approach which cinema designers, despite their later modernist pretences, never truly left behind. Most development was suspended when the First World War began.

By the 1920s, the United States had an unassailable lead in film production and, with the advent of talkies, American influence began to be felt in the design of cinemas. Lanarkshire folk preferred the escapist Hollywood romances, lavish musicals and fast-shooting Westerns to British productions and soon American art deco was influencing cinemas in Lanarkshire as elsewhere in Britain. New cinema buildings were given evocative names like the Broadway (Blantyre), the Ritz (Strathaven) or the Roxy (Hamilton). The latter was a shoddy hall with bare roof trusses which failed to live up to the grandeur of its 6,000-seat namesake in New York, the world's biggest and most luxurious cinema. By the late 1930s there were sleek, tiled 'super' cinemas in the 'streamline moderne' style, boldly outlined at night in brightly coloured neon, with their advertising hoardings carefully placed to attract the attention of tram and bus passengers. A greater contrast to the dour and soot-stained sandstone terraces whose streetscene they often shared would be hard to imagine.

Not all of Lanarkshire's cinemas were glamorous and modern, though. A few were appalling. Archie McNeil, who worked as a doorman in the Pavilion, Uddingston during the 1940s, recalls:

> In Lanarkshire, cinemas were rarely short of audiences, and if they were doing badly, it was their own fault. Some of these places were just flea pits. In fact, big circuits like Gaumont and Odeon were often the worst offenders as cinemas – in what their head offices must have considered remote places like Coatbridge and Bellshill – were the last ones to have money spent on them. You never were in such filthy, draughty places as the Bellshill Picture House or the Motherwell Pavilion, both run by Gaumont.

John Duddy, who was chief projectionist at the Rialto, Airdrie, in the early 1950s remembers that:

Next door to the Rialto in Hallcraig Street was La Scala, which occupied the old town hall and had ancient projection equipment. One night the picture stopped suddenly and, as usual, the audience responded with pandemonium. The chief's voice was heard through the projection porthole, shouting back 'It's no a break-doon It's NO a BREAK-DOON!, ma jaicket's stuck in the machine'. As the projection box was built in the rear stalls, this chief had a habit of using his oil can to squirt in the face of inquisitive heads which blocked the light path to the screen. He got his comeuppance when one evening a packet of greasy fish and chips came flying through the porthole and caught him square on his bespectacled face.

The Whifflet Picture House, later known as the Garden, had the screen painted on the rear wall and sound equipment made by a man called Guest. When I commented to a Western Electric sound engineer that Mr Guest never seemed to touch the inside of the amplifier, his reply was 'He's frightened to – there's nae insulation on the wires in places'.

The entrance to the BB (Bright and Beautiful) Picture House in Coatbridge was a single doorway with a narrow passage and a pay box, leading to a hall with wooden rafters and panelled walls. There were no dimmers for the house lights, so the flick of a switch put the auditorium into total darkness until the film leader began. There were no curtains either and smelly gas secondary lighting, so weak your eyes hardly noticed it.

The BBs, as it was known, was a Gaumont cinema. The three big national circuits – Gaumont British, Odeon and ABC were all well represented in Lanarkshire, although the finest cinemas in the area usually belonged to independent companies. The Regal in Lanark was typical. A cinema magnate, in this instance Sir Alex King, would form a company with well-known local businessmen, who issued shares to cover the cost of construction. These locally-owned cinemas were hailed as important civic amenities and they offered many patrons the unaccustomed luxuries of fitted carpets, concealed colour-change interior lighting and several sets of embroidered and festooned curtains over the screen. The romance of the movies affected every aspect of their design and operation. The travelling showmen, in particular, used great ingenuity when building their own permanent cinemas. In Carluke, Mickey Burns used lavish interior panelling, rescued from a scrapped liner, to embellish his Windsor cinema, while John Sheeran rescued the first class dining saloon from another to line the auditorium of his Rex in Stonehouse.

When the Second World War began, materials rationing was imposed and an embargo was placed on cinema construction. Somehow, the mighty Green's Playhouse in Wishaw, Lanarkshire's largest cinema with 2,982 seats, was completed in December 1940, but another interesting project, the State in Bellshill, was abandoned once the steel frames were erected. It was not until 1951 that the site – having been sold in the interim to George Palmer – was completed as the luxurious George. Inspired, it is said, by a visit by Palmer to the prestigious flagship Odeon in London's Leicester Square, the George was thought to be a modern wonder with its dramatic exterior in tiles and glass block-work, its striking streamlined interior and its stereo sound system, which was reportedly the first in the district. George Palmer was Lanarkshire's most significant cinema owner, with venues all over Central Scotland and Ayrshire too.

Television began to make serious inroads in cinema attendances during the 1960s. Hollywood meanwhile produced more adult-orientated films, whose depiction of sex and violence, however tame by today's standards, invariably attracted an X certificate, preventing children and young teenagers from gaining entry. The image of the cinema as a comfortable and friendly resort, to which the whole family could escape and dream a little, began to fade. Fights and vandalism made some of the declining picture palaces nightmarish to manage and inevitably deterred respectable patrons. Green's Playhouse in Wishaw seems to have been particularly badly affected. As audiences declined, cinema owners found that they could make more money by switching from films to bingo, and the 'numbers game' has saved many of Lanarkshire's most interesting cinemas from early demolition. However, these buildings were never intended to last forever and many have not survived. Rather, their design captured the aspirations of popular taste for a brief phase before falling slowly out of fashion.

Today, new multiplex cinemas are opening all over the country. As with the recently-opened Showcase in Coatbridge and Arrow in Wishaw, they have until now been built as elements of out-of-town retail or leisure parks with bowling alleys, bingo halls and burger restaurants often sharing the same site. They are accessible only by car. Their architecture owes more to that of supermarkets or furniture warehouses than the lavishly conceived cinemas of old, the theory being that today's audiences only come for the film and not the atmosphere of the cinema building. While they are neither architecturally distinguished nor such an integral part of the community as before, these new cinemas at least offer a bewildering choice of programmes under one roof and are spearheading a revival in cinema-going. Now is an appropriate time to look back to the remarkable design and social history of the cinemas which have delighted generations of Lanarkshire folk.

As the photographic record of Lanarkshire's cinemas is patchy and some were simply converted from miners' welfare and other halls, this volume is not intended as a comprehensive gazetteer. Rather, it is a record of Lanarkshire's more interesting cinema buildings. The towns are arranged alphabetically and the cinemas are illustrated chronologically within that framework.

La Scala was an unlikely name for the attractive former town hall in Hallcraig Street, with its Scots baronial castellated frontage with crow-step gables. Run by J. J. Bennell's BB (Bright and Beautiful) Pictures from 1906, it became the Coliseum cinema in 1928, managed by the Glasgow-based Pennycook circuit, and was sold to the Allan Brothers, who renamed it, in 1938. La Scala was destroyed by an overnight blaze in 1957 and the building was demolished.

Developed by a local firm to a design by James Davidson of Coatbridge, and opened in February 1920, the New Cinema was the largest of Airdrie's four picture houses. It was modernised in 1938 with a smoothed facade and was further rebuilt in 1955 when it became the first Airdrie cinema to fit a wide CinemaScope screen – an expensive installation which involved the extension of the auditorium to the rear. The New Cinema was run latterly by the Paulo family and was demolished in 1980. A new road runs through its site, although the rest of this scene has changed little over the years.

Built in 1856 to a James Thomson design as Airdrie's Corn Exchange Hall, this fine corner building, grandly crowned by the town crest, soon became an indoor market to which showmen brought their stalls. In 1908 it was converted to the Hippodrome Theatre, a popular variety venue where Harry Houdini famously performed his escapology act on the front steps to a crowd of thousands. It became a cinema during the First World War and was renamed the Rialto in 1929. Alex Frutin, the Glasgow cinema and variety impresario, ran it for many years until bingo took over in the 1960s.

The Pavilion, which started out as a roller skating rink and became a cinema and theatre in November 1911, was entered beside the Victoria Bar. It was run for many years by the Singleton circuit. When George Singleton received a generous offer from Odeon in September 1936, he sold his original chain of basic cinemas, including the Pavilion, and was able to build modern 'super' cinemas with the proceeds. The Pavilion's biggest scoop was to show the Technicolor version of the Coronation film *A Queen Is Crowned*, while larger rivals made do with the inferior black and white version. When it put on CinemaScope films, a wide screen was achieved by lowering the top masking, making the film smaller than normal and defeating the point of the process. Being small and quaint, the Pavilion never took the Odeon name and was disposed of to Classic in 1967. The site was cleared in 1973 to enable the erection of the new sheriff courthouse.

The former Bellshill Theatre, designed by Thomas Martin in 1905, was converted to the Picture House in 1911 by the Motherwell-based Thomas Ormiston circuit. The circuit was taken over by a Gaumont British subsidiary, Denman Picture Houses, in 1928. The 629-seat Picture House must have been one of the dullest Gaumont-owned buildings. It closed in 1958, not so much a victim of television as of competition from the modern and luxurious George cinema across the road.

Opened in 1923 by a local syndicate chaired by Mr Antonio Verrecchia, the proprietor of the neighbouring ice-cream parlour, the Alhambra was the cinema where George Palmer made his reputation, first as manager, then as a director and eventually as sole owner. The 1,300-capacity venue was extensively rebuilt in 1938 with new luxury seating, marble in the foyers and two sets of embroidered screen curtains. The neon outlining the facade made the Alhambra a landmark which could be seen from as far away as the platform of Mossend Station. After bingo use failed, it was demolished for housing in 1995.

Described by the *Bellshill Speaker* as 'Lanarkshire's Wonder Cinema', the George finally opened on 24 November 1951. It had been planned as early as 1938 by Harry Bradley, a Kirkconnel-based showman, and was originally to have been called the State. George Palmer bought the site and had new plans drawn up by Lennox D. Paterson, but wartime building restrictions initially led to delays. However, Palmer recruited the support of the all-powerful National Union of Mineworkers, with whose backing the necessary building certificates were granted. The exterior was a startling addition to Bellshill's grimy streets, with a futuristic tiled frontage outlined in pink and blue neon and a tower of internally-lit glass bricks at one end. Within, the George was equally striking. The entrance doors, without frames, formed a continuous expanse of armour-plate glass, letting light flood out into the street. The 'GP' logo was set in mosaic in a cream and green terrazzo floor, while concealed lights shone overhead.

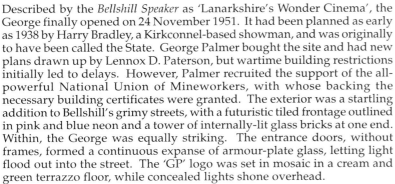

The manager of the George was Bill McGhee, a long-time associate of George Palmer. He is seated front centre in this picture, flanked by cashiers and usherettes, with Mrs Palmer behind him. The projectionists are in the back row. Cinema managers were popular and often revered figures in the local community and had to possess many talents, from doing accounts to hosting Saturday morning kids' matinee shows.

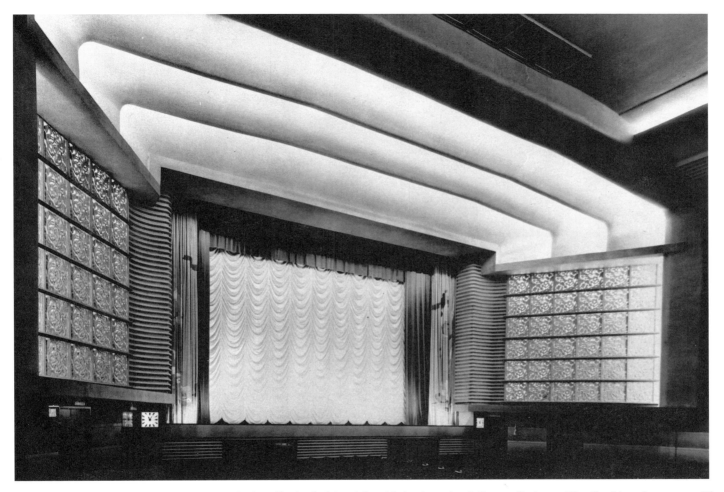

The auditorium of the George, which seated 1,750, had walls shaded in pink with intricate back-lit ventilation grilles flanking the screen. There were long troughs of concealed lighting in the ceiling, and three sets of curtains. First, the lights dimmed from the rear to the front and the grilles darkened, then the turquoise house curtains with their brilliantly coloured tropical fish opened. Behind, there were crimson velvet ones and a silver festooned screen tab which lifted to reveal the vast 'Miracle Mirror Screen'. The George was sold for bingo in the early 1970s, but a licence was refused and it continued as a cinema until demolition in the autumn of 1982.

Known locally as 'The Dookit', the Picture House was opened in 1913 for E. H. Bostock's circuit. When sound equipment was installed in 1929, the building was leased to the Glasgow-based L.C.V. circuit, which belonged to a Mrs H. W. Urquhart. It closed in the early 1960s and was later demolished.

A.6546. GLASGOW ROAD, BLANTYRE.

The 1,118-seat Broadway in Glasgow Road opened in September 1939 when Errol Flynn was the big attraction in *The Dawn Patrol*. As war had been declared it was nearly requisitioned as a Civil Defence depot, but the authorities felt that its role as a local morale-booster was more important. It was run by the Ayr-based Blantyre Picture House company at first, then by Jack Brown, a Glasgow cinema and ballroom entrepreneur, from 1969. The Broadway was closed in the early 1970s and later demolished.

The Empire, conveniently located by the tram terminus in Main Street, was the least glamorous of Cambuslang's cinemas, known locally as 'The Bug Hut'. Being independently owned, it was unable to secure the latest films and tended to show revivals of Westerns and musicals with cheaper prices of admission. The Empire was a casualty of TV and closed in the early 1960s, although the building survived in a state of increasing decay until 1984.

Of Cambuslang's three cinemas – the Ritz, Empire and Savoy – only the latter still stands, surviving as a Vogue bingo hall. The Savoy was built in 1928 for a local firm and was designed by John Fairweather, who created the famous Green's Playhouses. It shares their classical styling, with columns along the sides of the auditorium.

The Ritz in Cambuslang was the only 'atmospheric'-style cinema in Lanarkshire. The facade was dull – an arch set between shop units, but the interior, by William Beresford Inglis, was remarkable, with three-dimensional Spanish buildings and plaster foliage around the side walls and a smooth plaster ceiling resembling a summer sky. The 1,595-seater was built in 1930 for ABC and was demolished in 1960 to make way for shops and offices.

In 1937 Mickey Burns, a flamboyant Irish showman, developed the Windsor adjacent to the site of the burned out Empire, fitting it out with interiors rescued from the Cunard liner *Mauretania* which had been scrapped in the Forth. The brick exterior represented a Moorish fortress of sorts with defensive walls, battlements and a gatehouse, topped by one of the glazed domes from *Mauretania*'s Winter Garden. The cinema was a dubious local landmark for fifty years and, although it has been demolished, Burns' house, which was in the same style, survives.

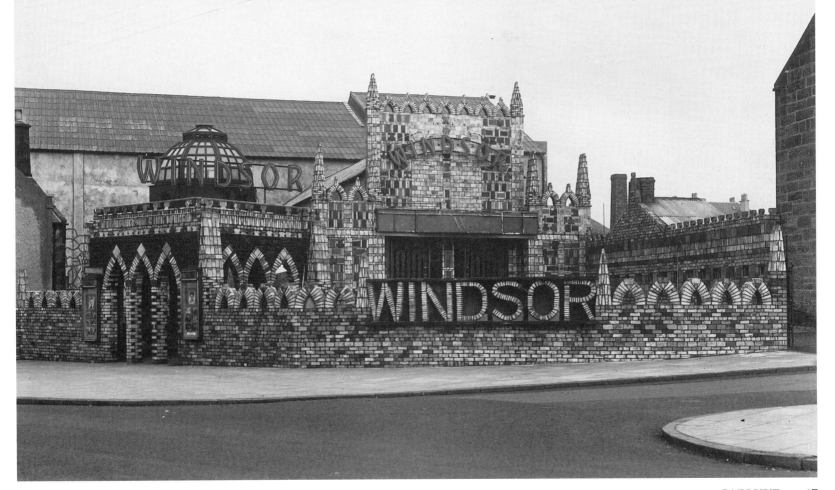

The foyer of the Windsor had panelling from *Mauretania*'s social hall and the row of Ionic columns with torches were more typical of Edwardian Atlantic liners than 1930s cinemas.

More ship timbers were used as dados in the 1,300-seat auditorium. The Windsor was sold by Burns to the Gourock Picture House Company after a dispute with a film renter who accused him of fiddling the box office takings. Burns went to the 20th Century Fox office in Glasgow and allegedly beat up the renter. Although he maintained his innocence, he was subsequently barred from receiving films by all the major distributors. The Windsor went over to bingo in the 1960s, but latterly fell into disuse. The derelict building was demolished in 1987.

Above: The Coatbridge Cinema, to the right of this view looking towards Langloan, was the first purpose-built picture house in the town and is seen here shortly after opening in 1913. It was also the first to fit talkie equipment in 1929 and the first to install magnetic four channel hi-fi stereo sound in the 1950s. Owned by a local syndicate, it continued in business until the mid-1960s. Today, the Time Capsule Leisure Centre faces the site where it stood.

Right: Originally a live theatre dating from 1914, the Empire quickly became a member of the Singleton cinema circuit. With the Airdrie Pavilion, it was sold to Odeon in September 1936 and renamed. It closed in 1976 with the film of the TV sitcom Dad's Army and was replaced by shop units. Both the Odeon and the insalubrious BB Picture House in Water Street (a former Gaumont property) came under Rank control in 1939, although the BBs closed in 1956.

The Theatre Royal opened in 1875 as a legitimate theatre and opera house. Designed by W. R. Quinton of Glasgow, the 2,000-seater had a dress circle, balcony and boxes with ornately gilded plasterwork and crimson drapes. There were frescoes of Shakespeare, Scott, Burns, Sheridan and Goethe in the ceiling. As tastes changed, the building became a variety venue in 1907 and, later, a cinema. In 1938 it was sold to the Harry Winocour Cinema circuit, and to Green's (of Playhouse fame) in 1956. John Duddy recalled a visit in the late fifties when it had declined considerably:

> 'The Theatre Royal was the only cinema to usher its patrons up to the 'gods', which were not only terrifyingly steep, but creaky as well. It was listed as a 1,000-seater at the time, but on all occasions I visited, I never saw a seat up there! The audience sat on the raised steps of the floor, looking at a wee screen at their feet, through a wire mesh safety fence. To make things worse, you often had to face the side because of the shape of the balcony, or had a pillar to block the view. They crammed hundreds of kids into the dark, dirty interior. Although the paint was blackened by nicotine and the chandelier had gone, you could just make out painted panels around the screen and ceiling dome. I recall seeing Lon Chaney Snr in a reissue of *The Unholy Three* there, billed as the man with a thousand faces . . . '

Largely unaltered since 1875, and totally unsuitable as a cinema, the Theatre Royal became the first casualty of the 1950s decline in attendances. It closed on 9 August 1958 and lay derelict until 1966, when it was demolished to enable road widening. Nowadays, the Jackson Street high-rise flats look down on the site where the Theatre Royal once stood in an area that has changed out of all recognition.

The Regal was one of a number of large ABC cinemas opened in Scotland in the 1930s to designs by Charles J. McNair and Elder, the distinguished and prolific Glasgow cinema specialists. The commodious 1,958-seater Regal opened on 17 February 1936 on a site facing the Cross and Central station. In this post-war view it has been fitted with the ABC circuit's distinctive triangular signage, which was intended to give the company's cinemas a clearer corporate identity and would have been lit in blue, red and green neon.

HOUSE, COATBRIDGE.   B.6071.

The interior of the Regal was notable for its use of concealed colour-change lighting, made by the Holophane company, which suffused the smooth walls and ceiling in slowly changing colours. It had twin pay-boxes in the foyer and crush halls which could accommodate hundreds, a considerable asset on cold and wet winters nights. Patrons who queued outside, thinking there were only 50 customers waiting, learned the hard way that there were actually 350. The Regal only had a narrow stage. Even so, amateur variety shows were given on Sunday nights when films could not be shown. Some were poor and heckling would ensue. John Duddy recalled one stand-up comic answering a restive crowd 'Ah ken a'm no worth much, but a'm worth whit a'm gittin' pied'.

In step with its owner's policy of further enhancing the ABC image, cinemas were renamed plain ABC with black letters in white lozenge-shaped signs from the mid-1960s onwards. Thus, the Coatbridge Regal became the ABC in 1963. Following the sale of the ABC company to EMI in 1969, their logo is also displayed. EMI subdivided the ABC in March 1973 to create a bingo club in the stalls and a small 510-seat cinema upstairs, a conversion which ruined the auditorium. The cinema section closed in 1983 and became a snooker club. The bingo area shut in 1996.

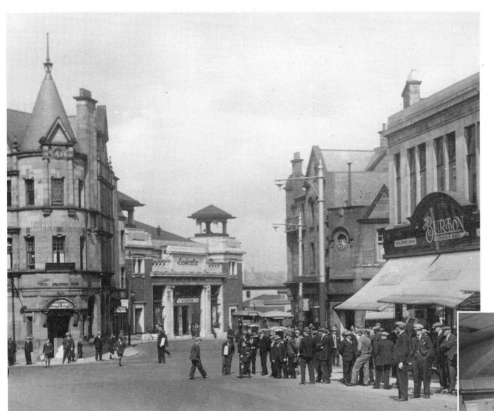

La Scala in Keith Street was opened in March 1921 by the Thomas Ormiston circuit. Designed by James McKissack, who went on to become one of Scotland's best cinema architects, its handsome twin-towered frontage in red brick with moulded faience dressings showed early promise. Faience was a hard-wearing terracotta which could be made in intricate shapes, and was ideal for use in grimy urban conditions as it could be washed clean. La Scala, seen here in the late 1930s, was sold with Ormiston's other cinema interests to Gaumont in 1928 and took the circuit name from April 1950. During the fifties it was famous for its children's matinees at which young patrons were encouraged to sing the Gaumont song: 'Every Saturday we come along wearing a smile/ Every Saturday we come along knowing it's all worthwhile/ As members of the Gaumont British Club we long to be/ Good citizens when we grow up and champions of the free!'

The Gaumont, as it was by then known, closed in November 1960. After a spell of dereliction, it became a bingo club and continued until 1997 as the Vogue. This 1996 photograph shows that apart from some bingo apparatus downstairs, the scruffy interior had changed little over the years. Following compulsory purchase, the derelict building is scheduled for early demolition as part of the regeneration of Hamilton's town centre, although the ornate frontage will be retained.

The gleaming white-tiled Plaza in Burnbank, a Hamilton suburb, was the first purpose-built Singleton cinema, remaining with the company even after the others had been sold to Odeon. It was built in November 1925 and continued until 1961, becoming a Top Flight bingo club. The frontage was modernised in plain brick and all trace of the old interior vanished at the same time. Having closed in 1996, the building, which bears little relation to how it looked in this splendid 1950s photograph, has lain derelict.

ABC's Regal opened on 17 August 1931 and its design by McNair was reported to have been derived from that of the company's flagship Regal in Glasgow's Sauchiehall Street. The cinema initially seated 1,800 and such was its success that in 1937 the balcony was enlarged to give a total of 2,023 seats. As with the Glasgow Regal, the interior was classical with pilasters and arches – originally containing murals of naïve landscapes – flanking the screen. In this early 1950s photograph these have been painted over.

The Regal was renamed the ABC in 1963, at which time a modern internally-lit film display sign was fitted above the doors and the cinema looked set for many more years of success. Unfortunately, it was badly damaged by fire in September 1976 and was never repaired. The shadow left by the ABC lozenge signs on the facade can still be seen. It has become a derelict eyesore and may soon be demolished as part of a town centre redevelopment programme – a sad lingering end for a once comfortable and popular cinema.

Having acquired a chain of rather basic, although very profitable cinemas when he took over the Singleton circuit in 1936, Odeon's hard-working founder, Oscar Deutsch, began a new building programme to get a bigger share of the lucrative Scottish market. In 1938 his London architect, Andrew Mather, was commissioned to design new Odeons at Hamilton, Motherwell and Ayr. These were reputedly the work of one of Mather's assistants, Thomas Braddock, and they certainly compared poorly with cinemas of the same size and vintage by Glasgow firms. The Hamilton Odeon, pictured when newly completed in November 1938, was at first entirely clad in cream faience tiles, but these soon began to fall off and were replaced by cement render. Notwithstanding its plainness, the Odeon has always been a popular and busy cinema. It was threatened with closure in 1976, but when the rival Regal burned down, it got a new lease of life and was instead tripled, reopening in May 1980. Nowadays, its three screens are slightly scruffy and it will be replaced by a new multiplex in the near future. At one time Hamilton could boast no less than seven cinemas. Apart from those already described, there was the Roxy, one block away from the Odeon in Townhead Street, and the Playhouse, known after the Second War as the Granada, in Quarry Street. The Playhouse, a former music hall, is now partly used as a Stepek electrical showroom. (The Hippodrome appears on the title page.)

This primitive shed of a cinema, the New Stevenston Picture House, opened in 1914 and was modernised in 1939 when it became the Regal. It is shown here shortly before closure in the early 1960s. The building lay derelict for years before demolition in the 1980s.

The Regal's modest facade (back cover) gave little hint that it was a large and well-appointed 1,316-seater cinema with cafe. As an important market town in the Clyde Valley, Lanark served a large hinterland and the Regal was always a prosperous cinema. The building was designed by Lennox D. Paterson of Hamilton for a local syndicate in which the respected Glasgow cinema magnate Sir Alex King was an important shareholder. Lord Dunglass opened it on 31 August 1936 when Charlie Chase in *Manhattan Monkey Business* and Laurel and Hardy in *The Bohemian Girl* were the big attractions.

Above the entrance there was a cafe. Cinema cafes were popular in the 1930s and were a sign of refinement. They offered elegant surroundings in which to enjoy luncheons and 'dainty teas' and were noted for courteous service and reasonable prices. Thus, they became havens for ladies meeting for a lengthy chat, and for children accompanied by mother meeting elderly aunts over a pot of tea. The Regal's cafe, with its splendid 1930s light fittings and rattan furniture, was typical. Such venues fell out of favour in the 1950s, when formica-lined self service cafeterias became popular.

The Regal was a fine example of a thirties 'streamline moderne' cinema interior with shovel-shaped light fittings and parallel coves focusing attention on the screen opening. It became a Vogue bingo hall in the 1970s, as pictured, but is still fully equipped and able to show films. The last regular film performance was of Kevin Costner in *Robin Hood – Prince of Thieves* in 1987. Lanark's other cinema was the Picture House, opened in 1913 by Thomas Ormiston. It became the Rio in the 1930s and was destroyed by fire in 1960.

Despite a population of only 14,000, Larkhall had two music halls. The Empire was a pioneering venture by George Urie Scott, a Glasgow cinema and theatre magnate. It was a typically sturdy brick hall with a small stage (no fly tower) and an ornate entrance portico. Inside, there was a single raked floor with wooden forms and partitions between the different price categories. There were two performances nightly with films shown on four nights from 1917. The Empire became a full-time cinema when talkie equipment was fitted in 1930. Inevitably it has become a bingo hall, confusingly renamed the Regal, and is a fascinating reminder of a lost era in entertainment.

Union St. Larkhall

The other music hall was the Grand Central in Union Street, which opened in 1909, seated 1,000 and became a cinema in 1914. Having been destroyed by fire in 1930 it was rebuilt as the modern Regal cinema. Its white stucco-clad facade did little to hide the ugly plain brick auditorium behind. The building was demolished after yet another fire and a Stepek shop now stands on the site.

Following the success of their travelling cinema shows, the Palmers, well-known Lesmahagow showmen, built this very basic wooden cinema in 1910. After several hair-raising fires, it was replaced by the Ritz in 1939. In the intervening period, and with the backing of local businessmen, a rival, the Glebe, opened in 1929.

It was cut-throat competition between the Ritz and Glebe cinemas in Lesmahagow. The Palmer's Ritz was designed and built by Stellmack and Co., an Ayrshire building contractor, and the lack of an architect's involvement showed in its severe exterior. A suspicious fire devastated the building only a few weeks after opening. With wartime building restrictions, the resourceful Palmers had to find materials for repair from other showmen. Robert Palmer recalls how a few weeks after reopening, youthful customers, who were known to be related to the owners of the Glebe, set fire to a row of seats in the balcony, but as the replacement floor was solid teak, the only wood the owners could lay their hands on, the building was saved. The Ritz closed in the late 1960s and was later demolished.

The Pavilion Theatre in Mossend (a linear mining village a couple of miles to the east of Bellshill) opened in 1912. In May 1937 George Palmer bought the building as his first cinema and, although the area was suffering from the effects of the Depression, spent £4,000 on a refurbishment which included a neon sign on the frontage displaying the venue's new name, the Regal. At the opening, he was presented with a leather dressing case by Bill McGee, the cinema's manager, who became one of Palmer's most loyal employees as he built up his circuit during the following years. In 1946 the Regal was destroyed in an overnight fire. (Scottish cinemas burned down with unfailing regularity, perhaps because, especially in industrial areas, some of their patrons had a macho disdain for the use of ashtrays).

BRANDON STREET AND CROSS, MOTHERWELL.   B.3264.

Designed by James L. Ross of Wishaw, La Scala opened in 1920 as an original member of Glaswegian John Maxwell's famous ABC circuit. (Maxwell was a staunch Liberal who later stood as the Motherwell candidate in the 1922 general election, during which, despite a stirring rally at which David Lloyd George spoke, he was soundly beaten by the Communist J. T. W. Newbold.) While the ABC company still exists under different ownership, the 930-seat La Scala survived only until 1959. In this post-war view, the advertising hoarding on the side wall shows ABC's distinctive triangle symbol. The solid-looking sandstone building was demolished and a supermarket now occupies the site.

Alec Cullen designed the handsome art nouveau-styled New Century in 1902. This postcard is one of several of the New Century written by an actress from London. She was evidently having a miserable time on her tour round Lanarkshire's variety halls, as on one card she complained to her mother that she was living in squalor: the roof leaked, there was no hot water, and Motherwell was, in her opinion, a 'miserable town with filthy streets'. After a bizarre tragedy in 1912 when a customer slit his throat during a children's pantomime, the building closed for renovation, becoming the Motherwell Theatre in September 1913 and operating as a cinema. Cinema shows were only a brief and unsuccessful interlude, however, and the theatre became the New Century again with drama and variety from 1915.

As Oscar Deutsch's Hamilton Odeon opened, across the Clyde Valley in Motherwell, his next venture neared completion. Opened on 31 December 1938, the modern 1,752-seater was immediately popular. Odeon was the first cinema chain to impose a recognisable corporate style on all its buildings, literature and advertising. Their Motherwell cinema, designed by Andrew Mather's London firm, was typical, with a cream tiled exterior, a small tower and the distinctive red name sign. Within, the Odeon-look extended to the design of carpets, ashtrays and the modish tubular-steel framed settees. An Odeon foyer would have been decorated in warming cream and peach tones with potted palms and portraits of film stars gazing down from the walls.

Unlike rival cinemas with their cafes and exotic designs, Odeon conceived their cinemas as 'machines for watching films', so the decoration tended to be sparse. This was entirely logical as films were shown in continuous performances and the audience rarely saw cinemas with the house lights on. In the thirties it seems that people didn't mind seeing a film from half way through to the finish and staying to watch the first half of the next showing. The Odeon became a bingo hall in 1975 and was pulled down twenty years later. At its peak, Motherwell boasted six cinemas – others were the New Cinema and the Empire, which was also used as a variety theatre.

The Empire, Shotts opened in 1912, run by a local firm in which the Marzella family, proprietors of the neighbouring cafe, were the major shareholders. It operated as a basic but popular cinema until the 1960s when it was sold to become a Top Flight bingo club. It is now part of a factory.

STATION ROAD. SHOTTS.

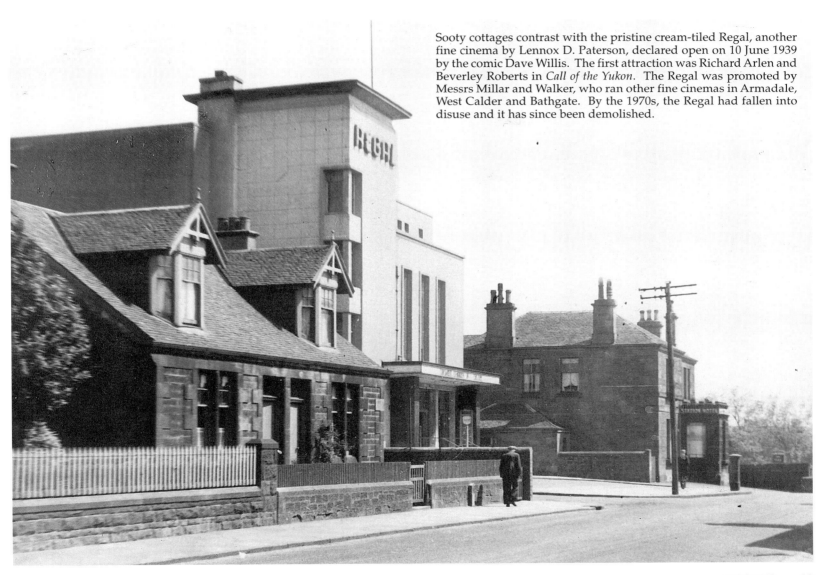

Sooty cottages contrast with the pristine cream-tiled Regal, another fine cinema by Lennox D. Paterson, declared open on 10 June 1939 by the comic Dave Willis. The first attraction was Richard Arlen and Beverley Roberts in *Call of the Yukon*. The Regal was promoted by Messrs Millar and Walker, who ran other fine cinemas in Armadale, West Calder and Bathgate. By the 1970s, the Regal had fallen into disuse and it has since been demolished.

Apart from its neon sign, the 509-seat Avondale in Barn Street was a most unassuming cinema. It opened in July 1930 and was initially run by a local firm, Strathbole Cinemas, which also managed the Ailsa cinema in Maybole.

Strathaven's cinema capacity more than doubled in 1938 when the Ritz was declared open by Sir Harry Lauder. Also locally-owned at first, the Ritz was quickly sold to Caledonian Associated Cinemas – once Scotland's largest independent circuit. By the 1950s CAC controlled both cinemas. While the Avondale, latterly known as the Dale, fell into disuse in the 1960s, The Ritz struggled on. It became a garage in the 1970s and has now been cleverly converted into a block of flats.

Although its exterior (pictured here with the owner and staff) dated from 1937, the history of the Rex's interior can be traced back to 1913 when the North-German Lloyd Steamship Co. ordered the Atlantic liner *Columbus* from the Schinau Unterweser shipyard at Danzig. The First World War intervened and the vessel was subsequently completed as the *Homeric* as a war reparation for the White Star Line. Built to replace *Britannic* (a sister of the legendary *Titanic*) which was sunk in the Mediterranean, *Homeric* was not a success, being too small and slow. She was sent for scrap at Inverkeithing in 1936. John Sheeran, a travelling showman, found some chandeliers from the liner in a Kirkcaldy flea market. He quickly made for the scrap yard where he bought the entire first class dining saloon to decorate the interior of the Rex, then under construction.

The *Homeric*'s ornate mahogany panels were brought to Stonehouse by train and re-assembled in the 750-seat auditorium of the Rex. The result was spectacular, and when Sir Harry Lauder opened the cinema on 22 January 1937 it was hailed as 'Lanarkshire's King of Picture Houses'. When visiting to promote a film, Jack Buchanan commented that the last time he'd seen 'that ceiling' he'd been eating dinner half way across the Atlantic! Business was brisk before the war, but when many villagers were conscripted away for war service, attendance declined severely. The Rex closed in the mid-1960s and, since re-faced, has become a warehouse for the Sheerans' amusement machines. The unique interior is still intact.

Wishaw's town hall was leased to E. H. Bostock and operated as the Pavilion from 1912, initially showing pictures and variety turns. It later became the Plaza and was sold to John Maxwell's ABC chain in 1927. The 1,074-seater closed abruptly in 1956 having been declared unsafe due to mining subsidence. It was demolished shortly thereafter.

Wishaw's next cinema venture was the Picture House, located in Main Street. It was opened by Provost Nimmo on 1 March 1913 for a local syndicate. Although early purpose-built cinemas such as the Picture House had fairly narrow frontages, they made the most of what space they had with pretentious neo-classical architecture, bold advertising displays and the seductive use of electric light bulbs to emphasise their entrances. Being lightly constructed, they were frequently modernised, and the Picture House was no exception.

These pictures were taken in the 1930s and show the queues in both directions that the Picture House attracted for *Treasure Island*. Although it had already been extended in the early 1920s, when this frontage was built, the work was still insufficient to allow it to cope with demand – especially following the advent of 'talkies' in 1929.

MAIN STREET, WISHAW.

In the summer of 1938, when business was slacker, the Picture House was closed for an unusual two-stage rebuild. First, the frontage was dismantled and a new tiled elevation with a tower and fluting, all outlined at night in red and blue neon, was erected to a design by Corrie and Millar of Wishaw. Such modern cinema designs certainly stood out from the sandstone tenements on either side. The following summer, the auditorium was modernised. The Picture House continued only until the spring of 1959 when its owners were made a generous offer for the site and it was replaced by shops.

Left: The Cinema opened in 1920 for the Thomas Ormiston circuit. Designed by a local architect, James L. Ross, the handsome 1,100-seater went to Gaumont in 1928 and became a Classic in 1967. The stalls were later converted to an amusement arcade and a small cinema continued to function upstairs. The building is now derelict and Wishaw folk go to the pictures at the modern four-screen Arrow Multiplex.

Above: The fourth and last of Green's mighty Playhouses opened in December 1940 next door to the Cinema, built as usual to a John Fairweather design. This was surely one of the most unsympathetic cinemas ever seen, with an ugly flank of plain brick running parallel to Kirk Road, brightened only by a colourful roof, tiled in stripes of red and green. As a Mecca Bingo Club the exterior is now a psychedelic orange and blue. Fortunately, the interior is still monumental with soaring Corinthian columns and a huge balcony, which even now retains two-tone seating. The original capacity was a staggering 2,982 and the entire space was finished in shades of gold. The tea-room had walnut panelling and throughout the carpets gave a fluorescent glow. Partly because of its size, the cinema proved difficult to manage and was plagued by vandalism in its later years. Bingo sessions eventually took over and the Playhouse has been well preserved, as shown here.